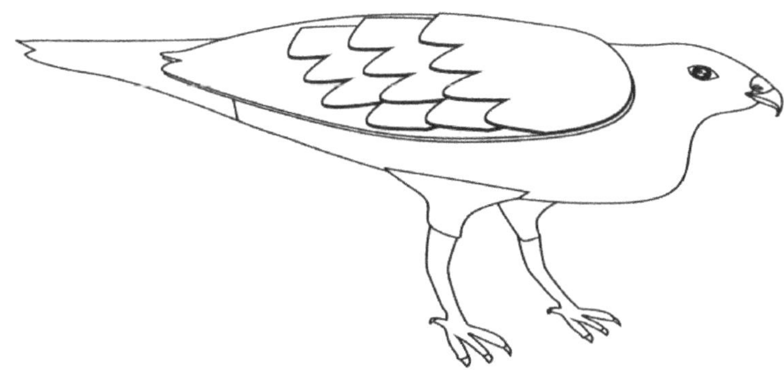

This coloring book belong to :

....

....

....

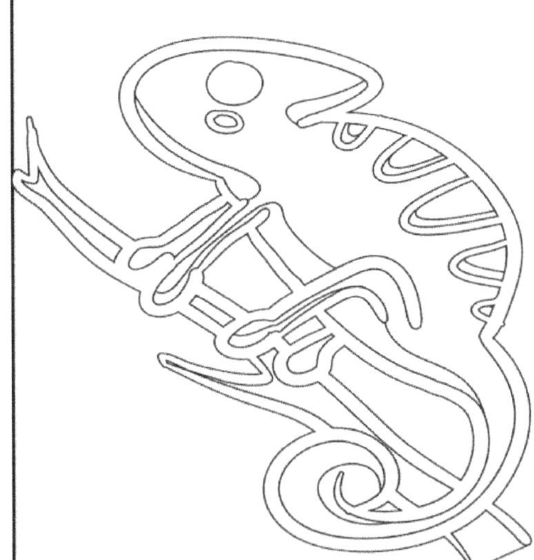

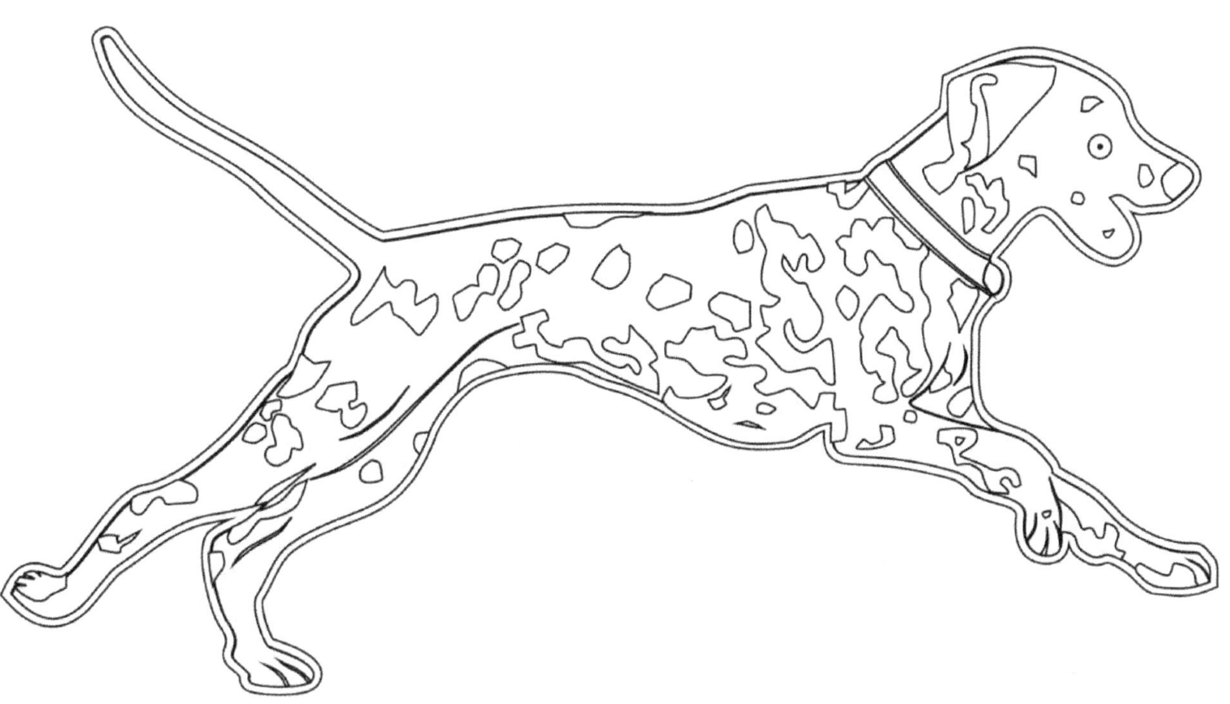

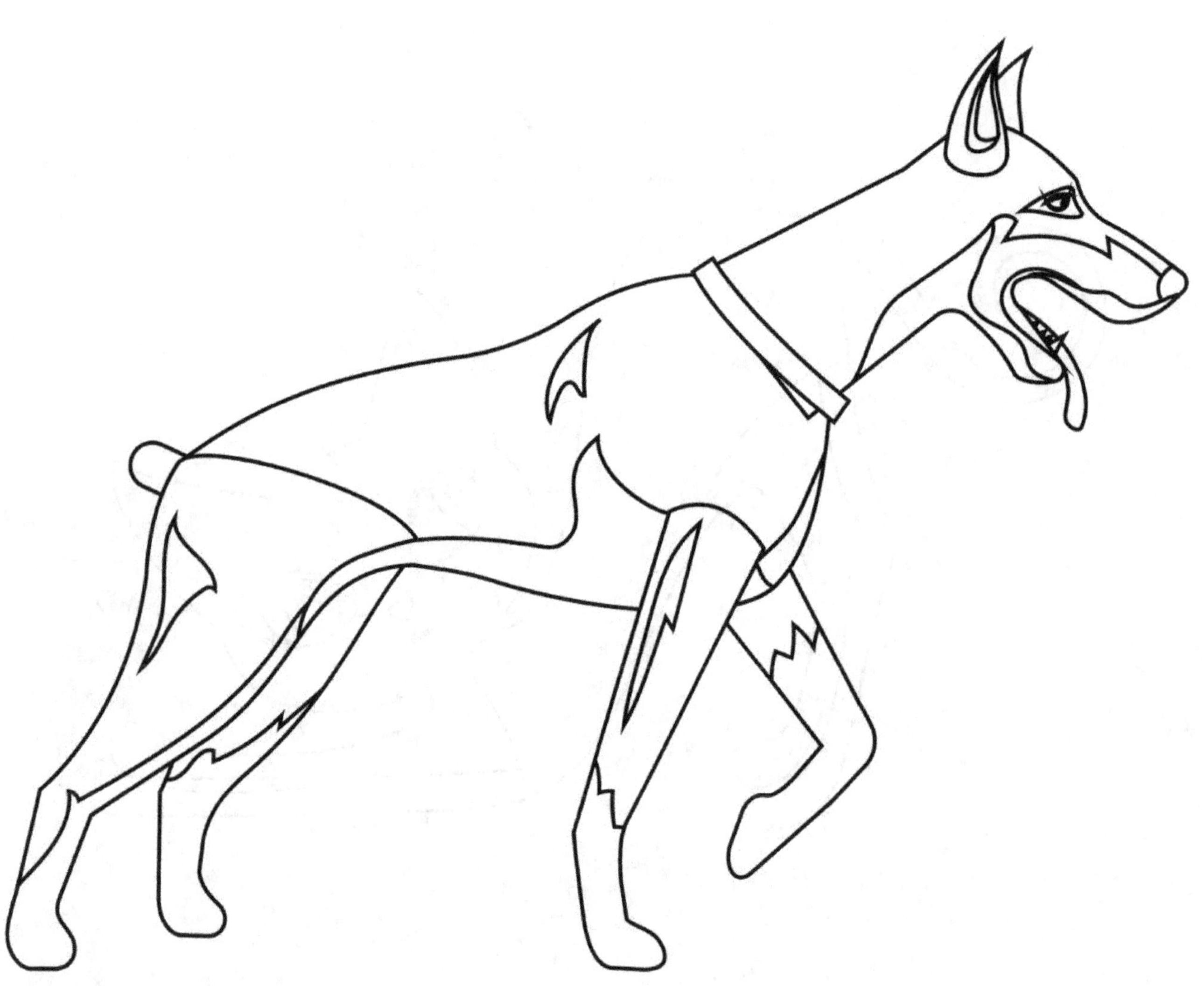

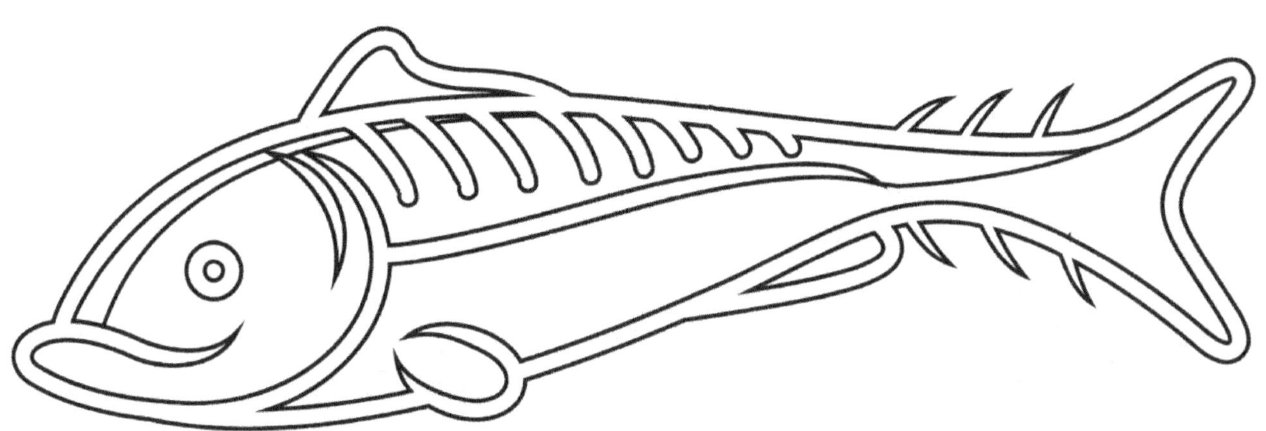

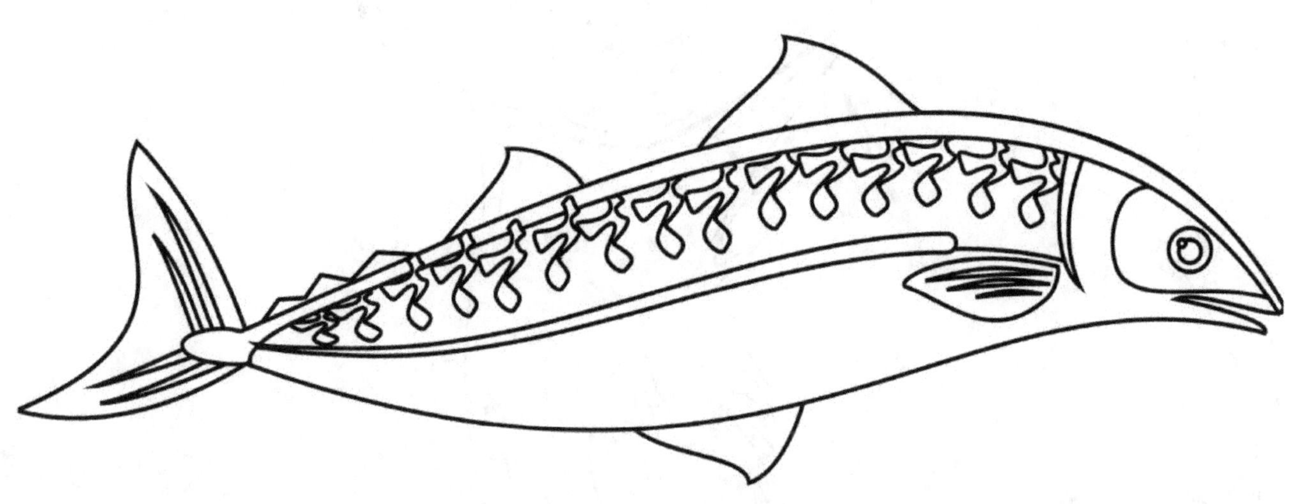

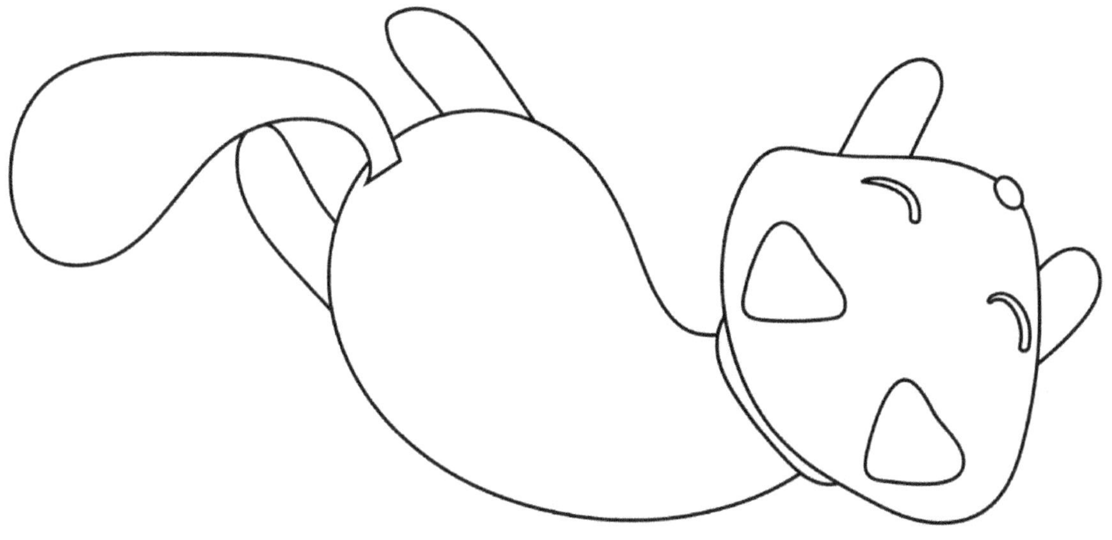

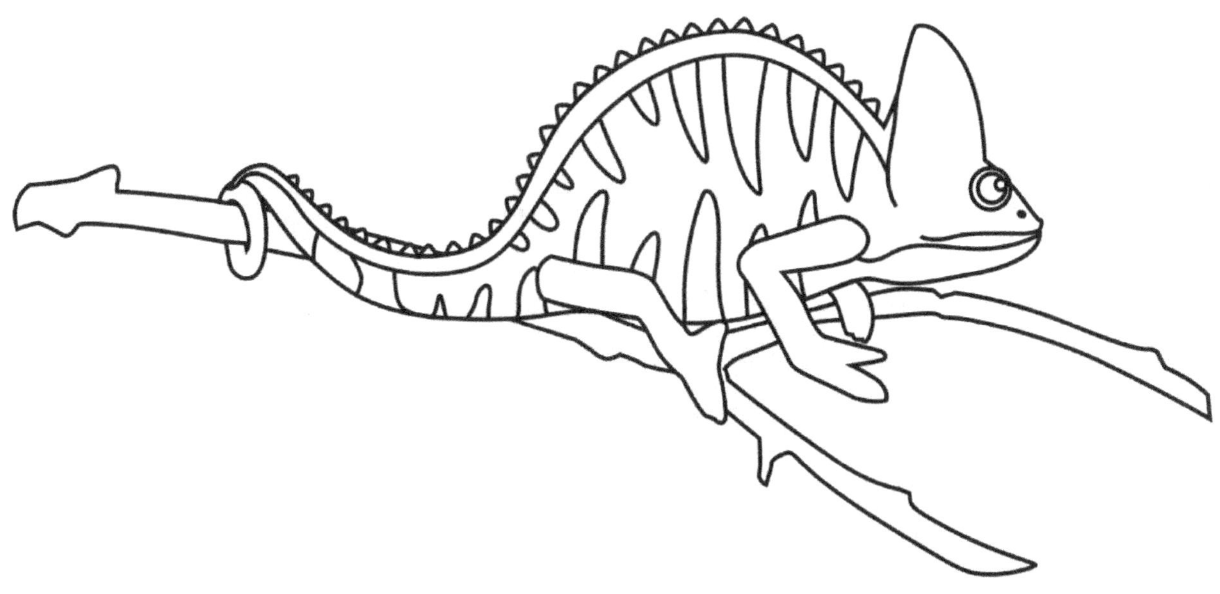

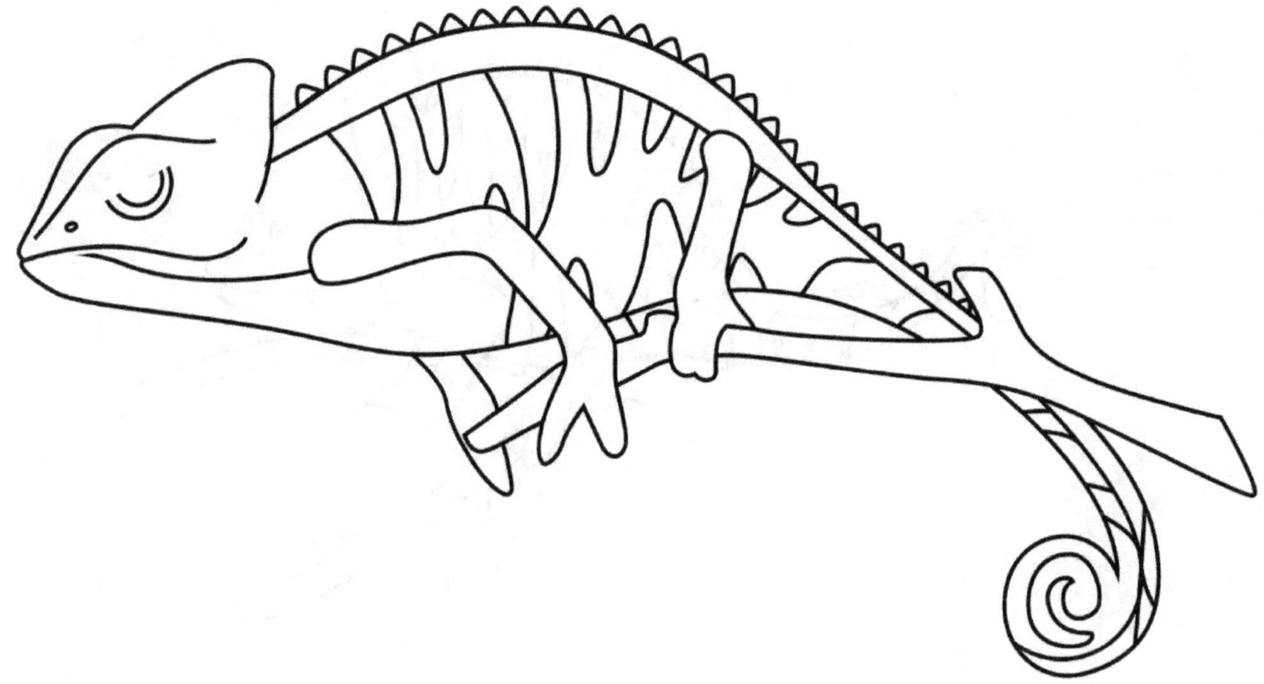

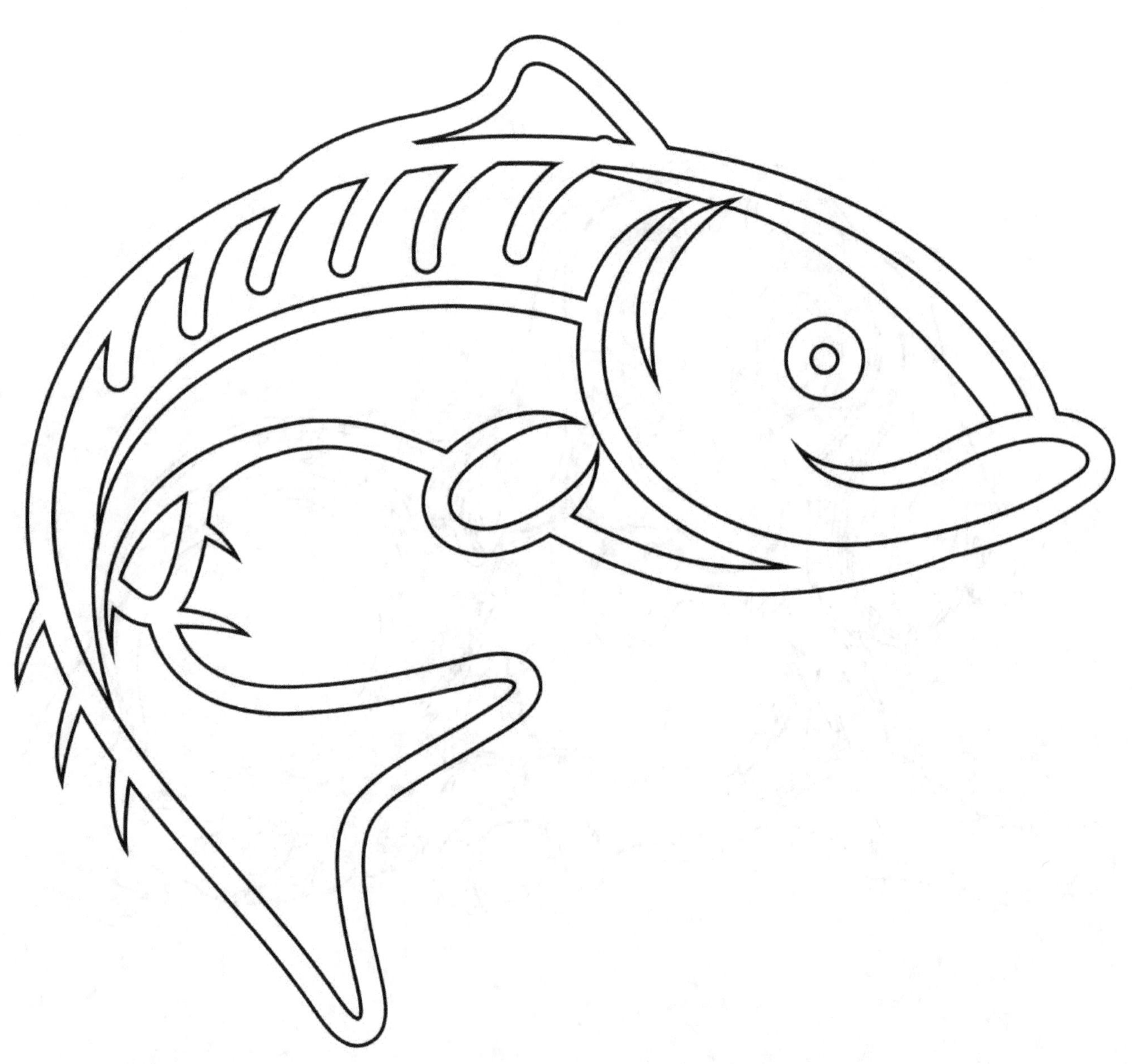

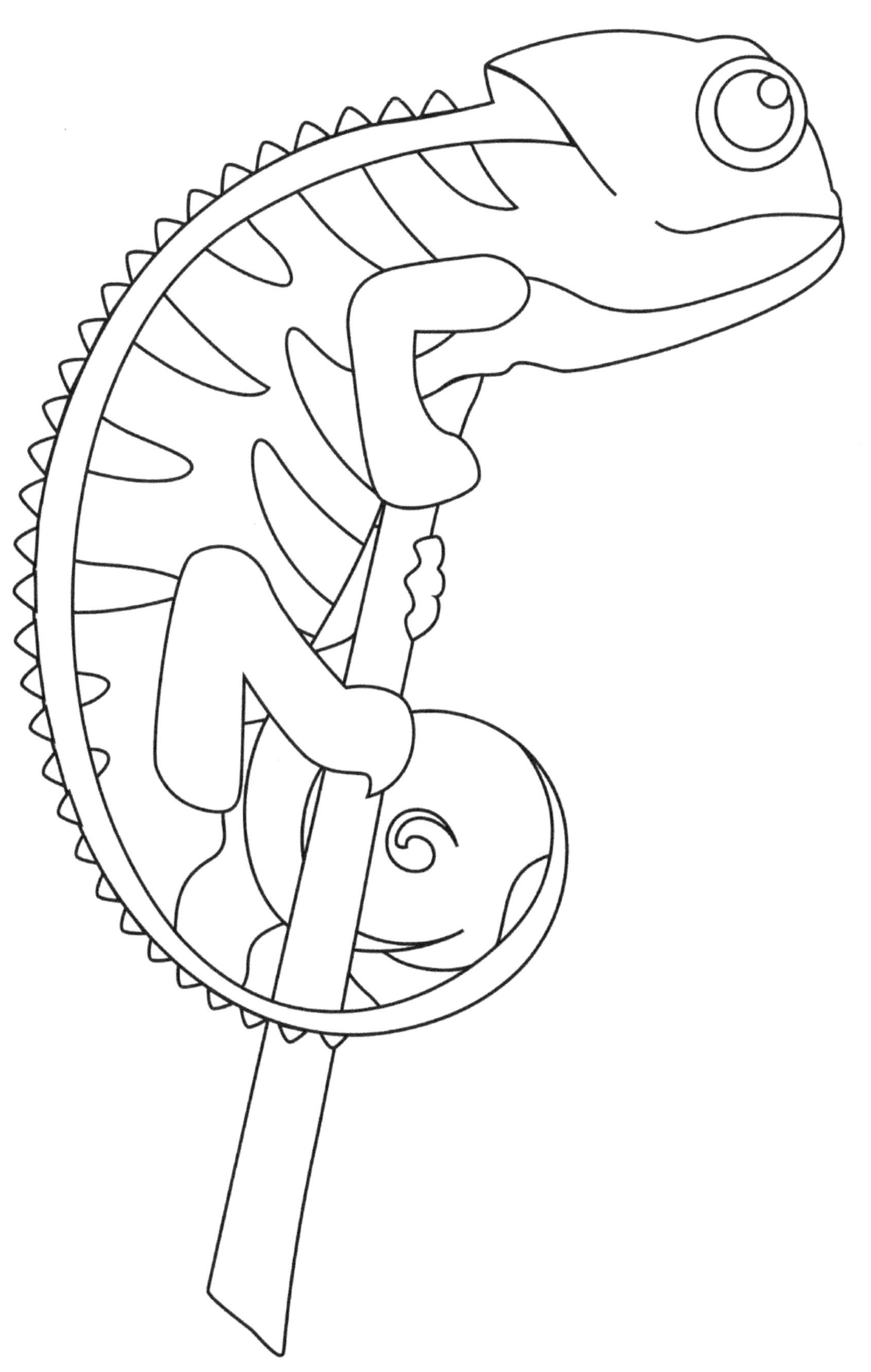

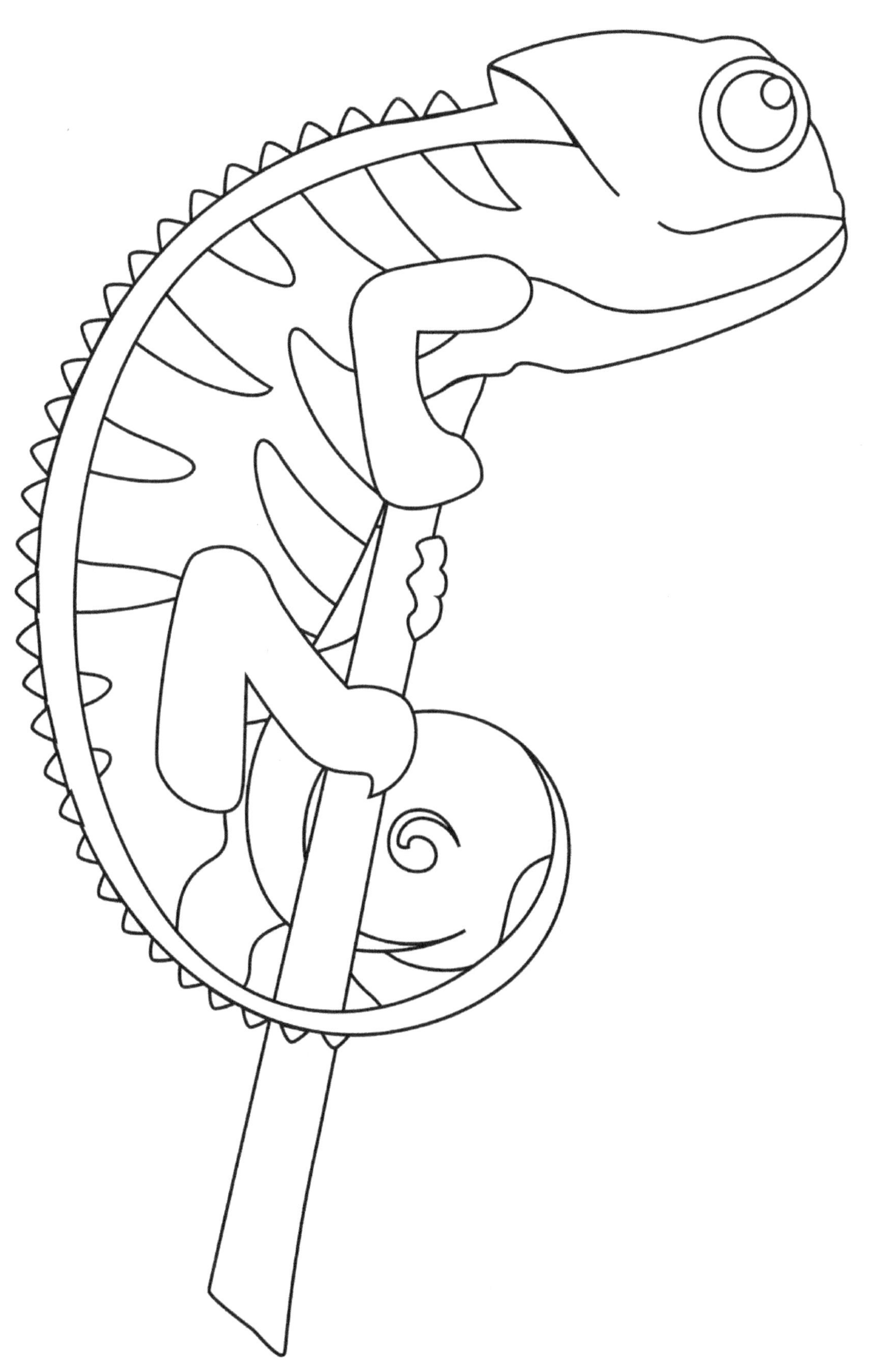

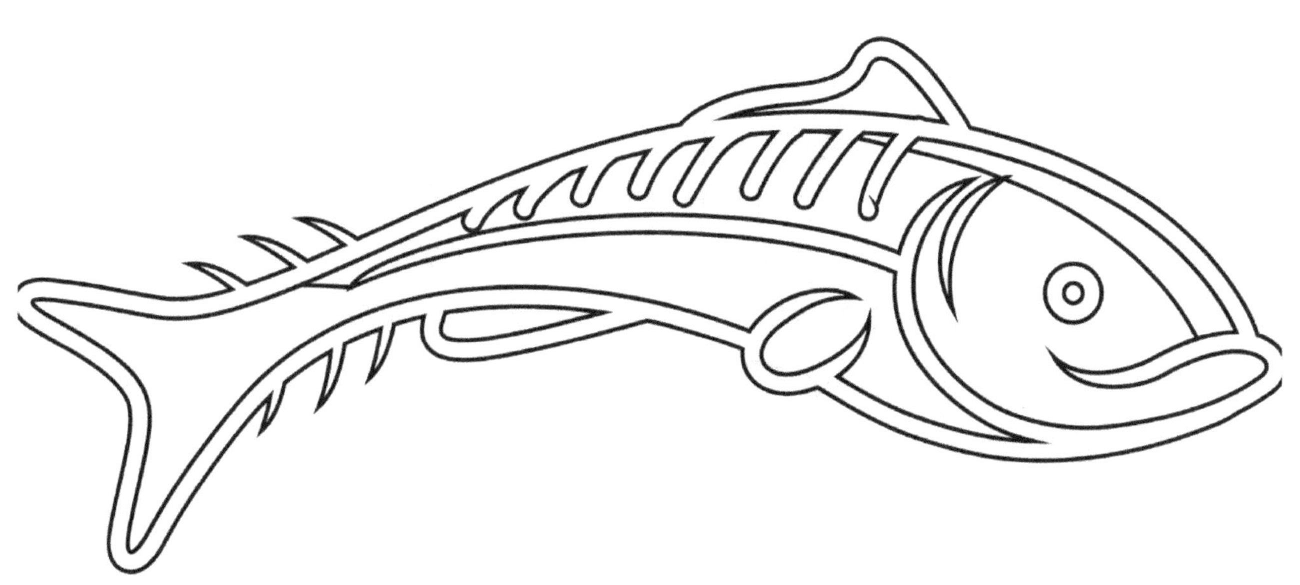

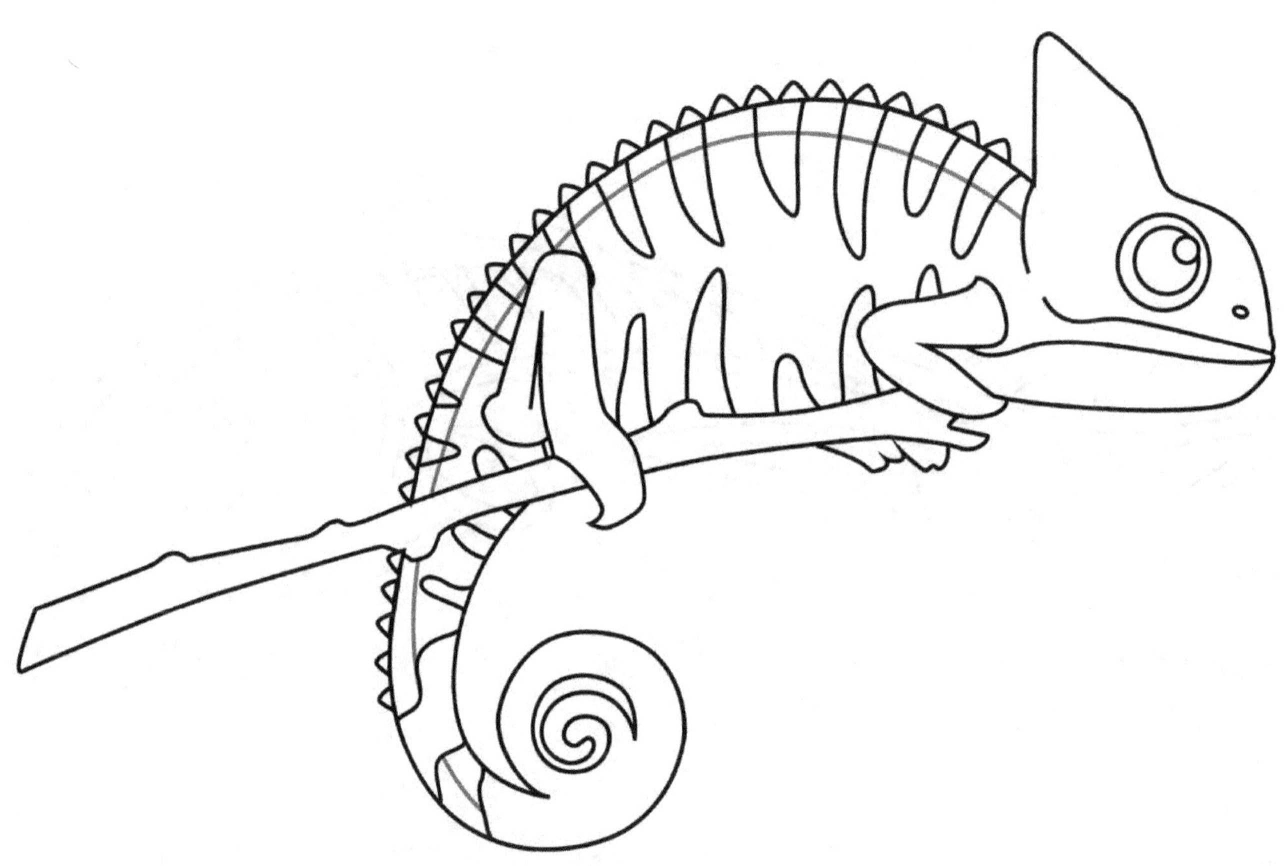

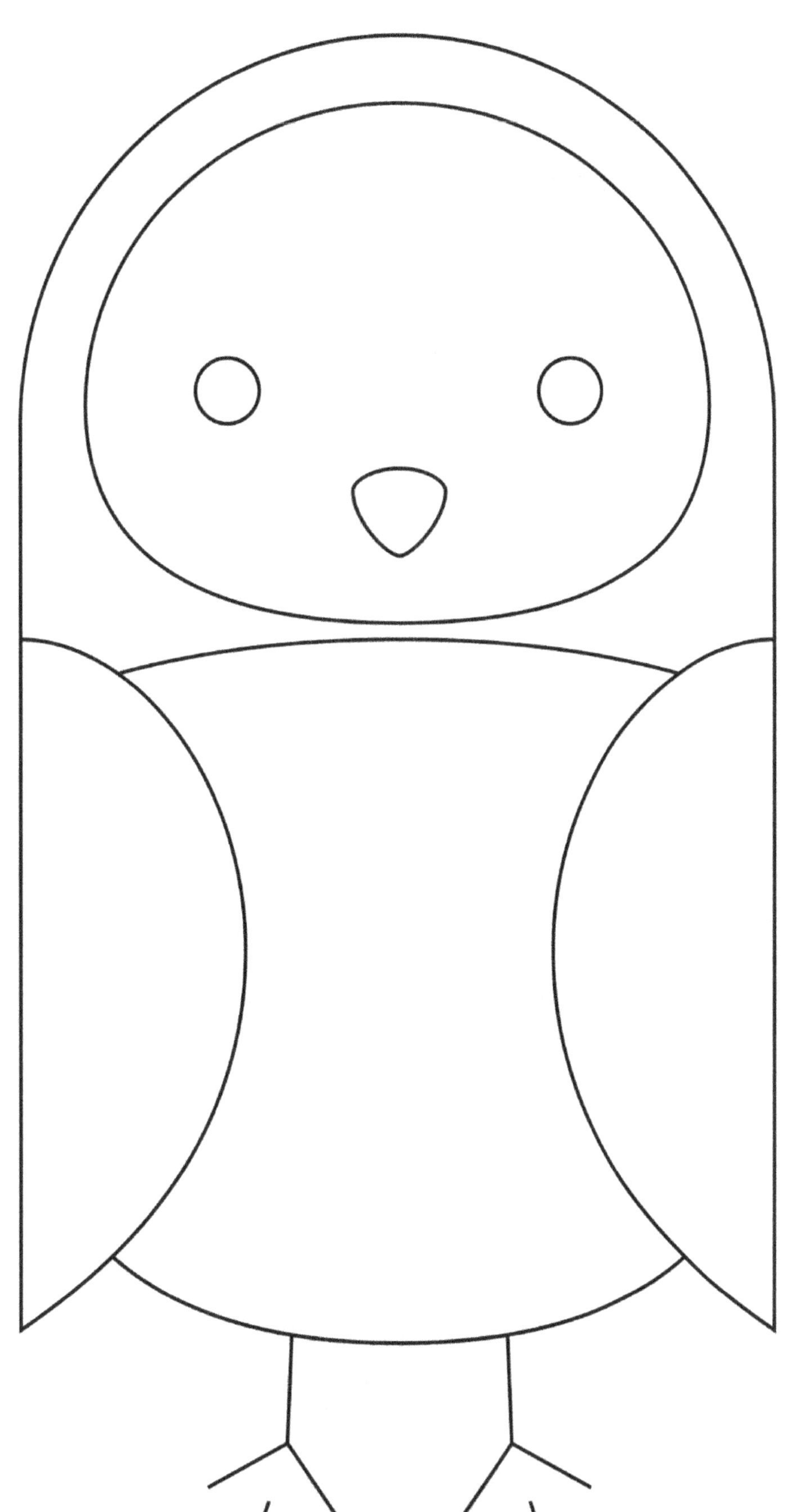

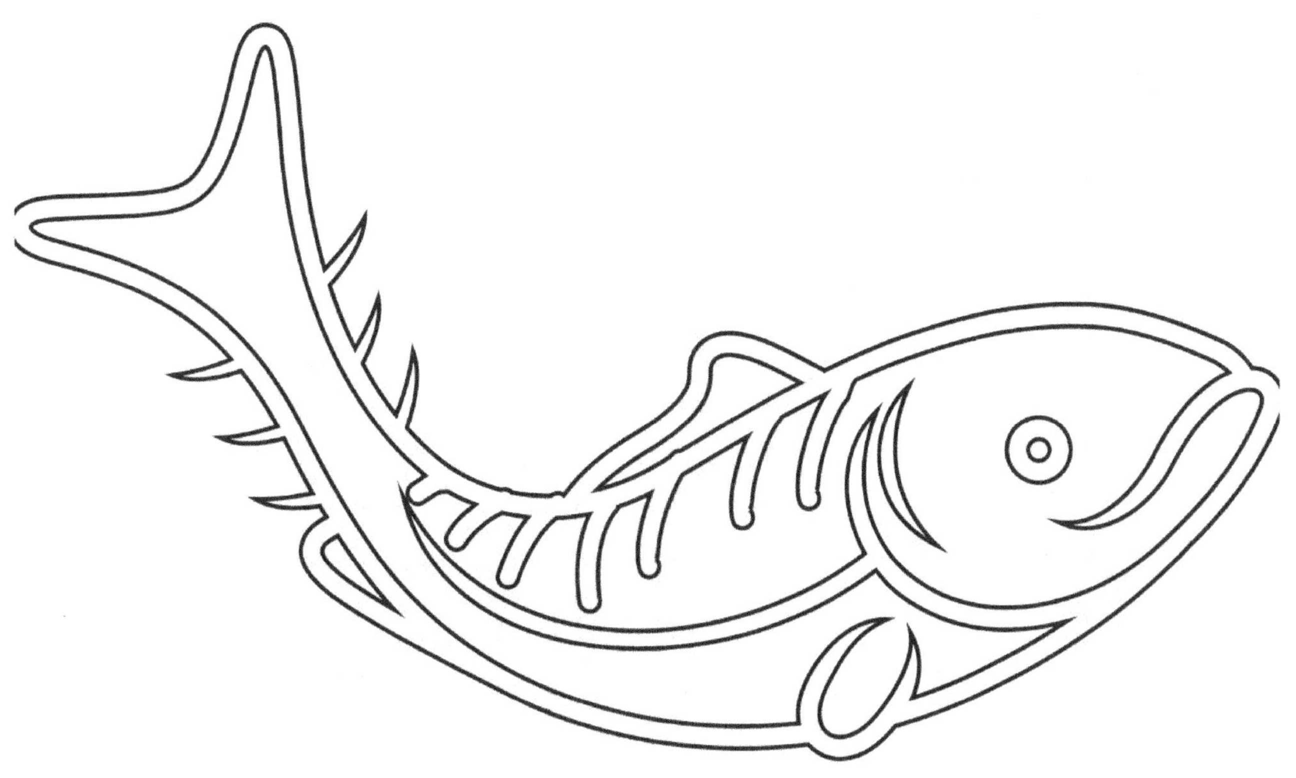

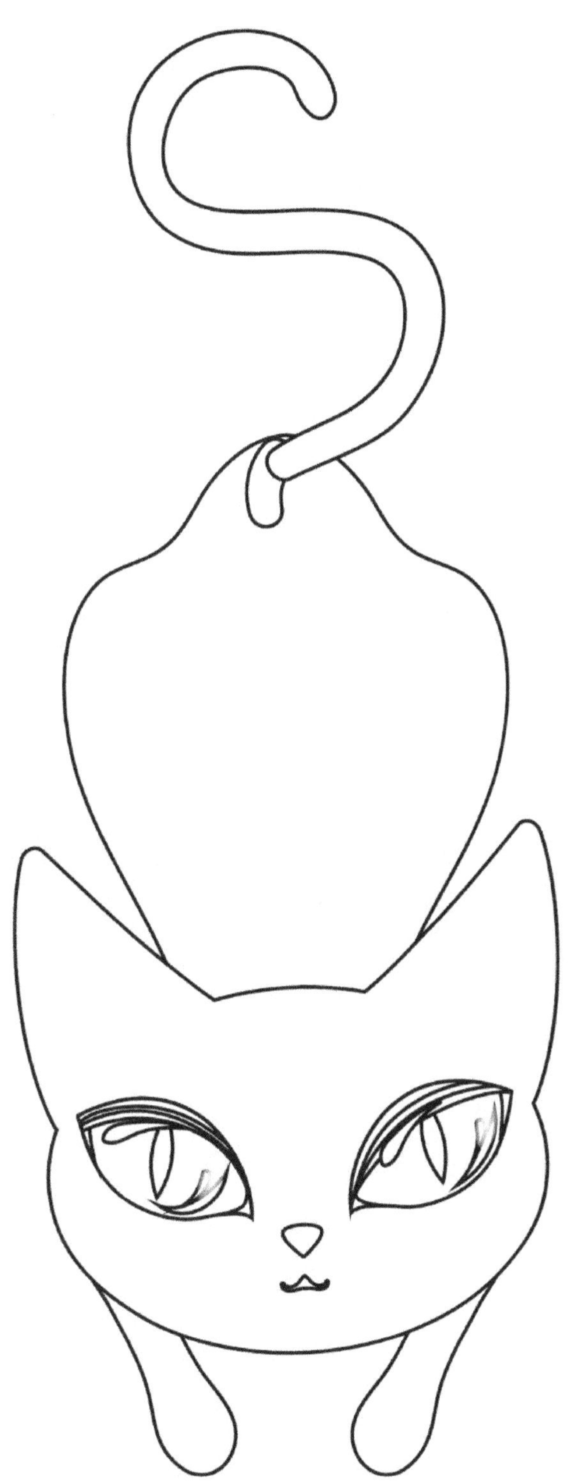

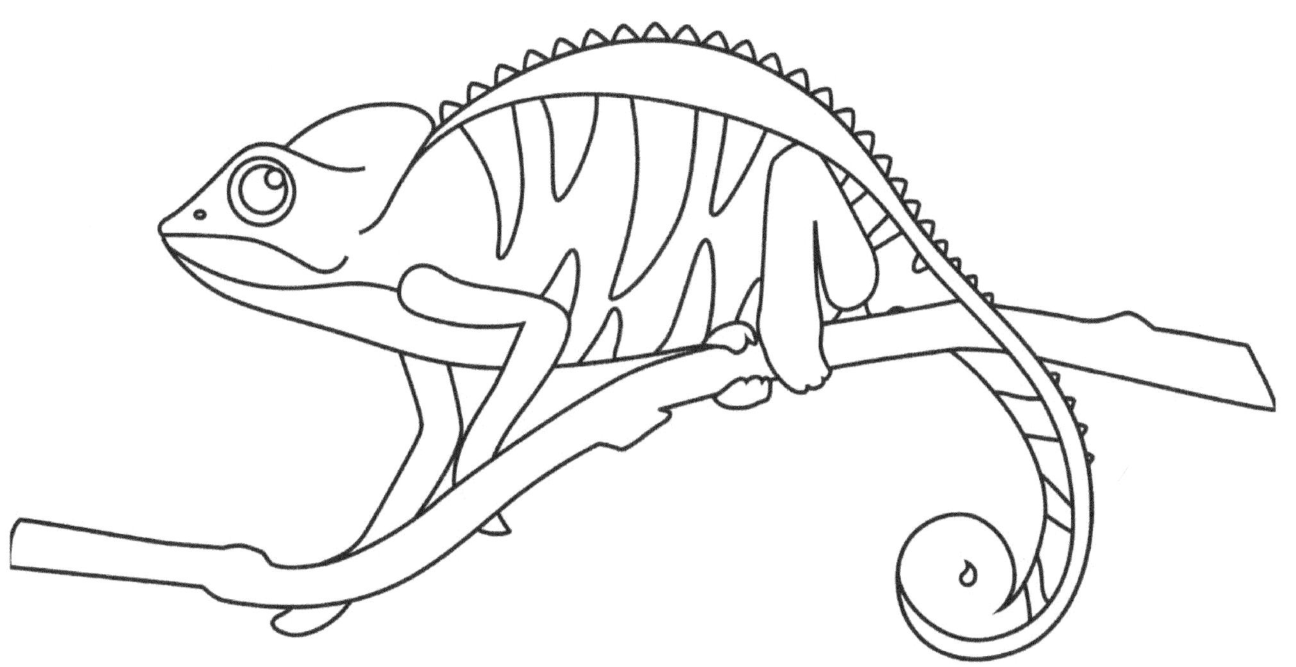